Vintage 94

League of
Canadian
Poets

National Poetry Contest

Over 16,000 poems have been entered in the League of Canadian Poets' National Poetry Contest since it began in 1987. These poems have shown the vitality and diversity of the poetry community in this country. The National Poetry Contest is the largest competition in Canada. The top 50 poems are gathered into an anthology each year. From these poems, the top three are chosen and cash prizes of $1,000, $750, and $500 are awarded.

Poems entered in the contest are unpublished and no longer than 75 lines. All entries must be typed, single-sided on plain 8 1/2" x 11" paper. As the contest is judged blind by a jury of poets, the author's name must not appear on the poem, but be submitted on separate sheet, along with an address and phone number and the titles of all poems entered. Copyright remains with the poet, but winners are asked to allow for the first rights to print their work.

There is an entry fee for each poem, and payment, either by cheque or money order in Canadian funds, should be included with the submissions. Deadline for the entries is January 31st of each year. Winners are announced at the LCP's Annual General Meeting.

Since the competition's inception, the winners have been:

1988 1st poem: Michael Redhill
        2nd poem: Sharon Thesen
        3rd poem: Cornelia Hoogland

        2nd poem: Stan Rogal
        3rd poem: Louise B. Halfe

1989 1st poem: Elisabeth Harvor
        tied: Elyse Yates St. George
        tied: Patricia Young

1993 1st poem: Joy Kirstin
        2nd poem: Patricia Young
        3rd poem: Gabrielle Guenther

1990 1st poem: Diana Brebner
        2nd poem: Blaine Marchand
        3rd poem: D.J. Eastwood

1994 1st poem: Tim Bowling
        2nd poem: John Pass
        3rd poem: Sue McLeod

1991 1st poem: Elisabeth Harvor
        2nd poem: David Margoshes
        3rd poem: Debbie Fersht

1992 1st poem: Nadine McInnis

For more information, please contact the League of Canadian Poets, 54 Wolseley Street, 3rd floor, Toronto, Ontario, M5T 1A5, tel.: (416) 504-1657.

Vintage 94

LEAGUE OF CANADIAN POETS

National Poetry Contest

Edited by Sandra Nicholls

QUARRY PRESS

Canadian Cataloguing in Publication Data is available.

Vintage 94, League of Canadian Poets

ISBN 1–55082–149–0

Cover art entitled *Stone Fruit* by P.K. Page,
reproduced from the oil pastel original,
by permission of the artist.

Design Consultant: Keith Abraham.
Typeset by Larry Harris
Printed and bound in Canada by Tri-Graphic,
Ottawa, Ontario.

Published by **Quarry Press Inc.**,
P.O. Box 1061, Kingston, Ontario K7L 4Y5.

Seventh National Poetry Contest
PRIZE WINNERS

First Prize
Tim Bowling
"Snowy Owl After Midnight"

Second Prize
John Pass
"Reprieve for the Body"

Third Prize
Sue McLeod
"When the Dog Dreams"

Contents

Preface

When I first agreed to be one of the jurors for the 1994 National Poetry Contest, I was ecstatic! Living in rural Nova Scotia with no decent bookshops for miles, the prospect of new poetry arriving at my doorstep from across Canada was unimaginably welcome. However, when the huge box arrived, containing nearly 1,000 poems (half of the entries), I wasn't as clear-minded. How was I going to read them all in time? What would my criteria be? And how would I explain my choices to my colleagues?

In the end, we were surprisingly close in many of our choices. Our focus seemed to be neither on technical merit nor emotional nor intellectual intensity alone, but rather, a capacity for wonder, a raw, dynamic energy, and, in some cases, a sense of humour. In this natural subjectivity, and dealing with so many entries, we may well have missed some fine poetry. But I believe the poems in this volume stand out on their own, and I also invite readers to select their own favourites from among them.

Tim Bowling's "Snowy Owl After Midnight" was a top choice, independently, of each juror, and so there was little discussion needed to make it our first-prize winner. For its incantory expression, for its attempt to grapple with an awareness not fully understood, and for the power of its imagery — "those moons / we watched in childhood," his "clipped, pale hands," and the closing image of the vigil which "burns white fire in the trees"— "Snowy Owl" lingered and resonated in all of our minds for weeks. It continues to pulse with an eerie power even as I read it now.

This groundedness, this turbulent but persistent hold on the earth seems to have characterized all three winners. John Pass' "Reprieve for the Body," our second-prize winner, offers the lusty, wilful manifest of the body, as it shakes off the "patient struggle" of the poem, "phooey / like a labrador," and stubbornly, joyfully, wistfully, or sullenly goes its own way, and despite the poet's calling, "won't come in for calling for the longest time." Wit, affection, and wonderfully unexpected images gave this poem the power to surprise, a rare and delightful quality.

Sue McLeod's "What the Dog Dreams" was another example of sheer wit and exuberance. What also impressed me about this work was the economy of language, the concise impact of lines such as: "Nights, he settles / and re-settles in the hollow rooms." From the opening image of the sleeping dog propped up "dog: side view," we laughed right along with the author, until we were brought to the poem's evocative conclusion, the inclusion of ourselves, transformed, in the dog's dream.

We decided to give Margo Button's poem "He Made Her Pregnant" an honourable mention after some heated discussion, and although it was a controversial choice, its raw power to provoke and to root itself in the jurors' imaginations made its impact impossible to ignore and worthy of special note.

The human mind is naturally inclined to look for patterns, and as I look at these poems I find several traits which link them: an attempt at illuminating or understanding another kind of awareness — the owl, the body, the dog; a steadfast refusal to lurk about in the dim rooms of the esoteric; a straightforwardness of language; and a comfortable hold on the endless curiosity of being human.

Because of space limitations I have only found room to mention the top prize winners, but there are many fine poems here, and I urge readers to take the time for all of them. It has been a pleasure for me to discover many new poets, to re-discover some I already know, and to get to know my fellow jurors: Fred Cogswell, Kay Tudor, and George Elliott Clarke. And now it's your turn: to settle in a comfy chair and make your own discoveries.

Sandra Nicholls
October 1994

Notes on the Authors

PEG BALFOUR was born in Sault Ste. Marie and lived there until 1990. The northern landscape has had an important influence on her poetry. She now lives in Kitchener and is a member of the Calliope Writers of Kitchener-Waterloo. She has won two Dorothy Shoemaker Awards for writers in Southwestern Ontario, a prize in a Wilfrid Laurier Shakespeare Contest, and an Amadeus Choir award. She is a graduate of the University of Toronto.

AMY BARRATT is a Montreal writer and co-founder of the Dead Beat Poets (Kingston-Montreal Axis). She doesn't have a driver's license.

JOHN BARTON has published several books of poetry, including *Designs from the Interior* (Anansi, 1994), *Notes Toward a Family Tree* (Quarry, 1993), and *Great Men* (Quarry, 1990). He lives in Ottawa, where he co-edits *Arc*.

JACQUELINE BELL is an Edmonton writer and visual artist. Her poetry has been published in *The New Quarterly* and *Dandelion*.

MAXIANNE BERGER is pursuing her M. A. in English Literature at Concordia University while continuing to work part-time as a clinical audiologist. Her Master's thesis will be a discourse analysis of 20th-century criticism.

JENNIFER BOIRE has been published in several small magazines, including *CVII*, *Poetry Canada*, *Room of One's Own*, and *Zymergy*. She wishes she could finish her Creative Writing thesis at Concordia University before 1995!

TIM BOWLING was born in Ladner, British Columbia the same year the Beatles invaded North America (they had more hair at the time). Now a hirsute poet, Tim's work has appeared in many journals, including *Queen's Quarterly*, *Poetry Canada*, *Grain*, *Arc*, *The Fiddlehead*, and *Capilano Review*.

RHONDA BRUCHANSKI would like to dedicate "trespasses and words of the cageling" to Yaweh, Ali, Winnie, Mirren, Santa, Kiwi, Phantom, Sushi, Zulu, Rico, Remy, Nelson, Licorice, Tao, Sinjin, Magnum, Ginger, and Jen.

MARGO BUTTON lives in Nanoose Bay, British Columbia. She is currently working on a long poem series about coming to terms with the loss of her son who was schizophrenic. She has had poems published in *Other Voices*, *CVII*, *Canadian Woman Studies*, *Dalhousie Review*, and *Prairie Fire*. She received Honourable Mention in the 1994 League of Canadian Poets National Poetry Contest.

JENNIFER CHEW is a student at the University of British Columbia. She was runner-up in the Orillia International Poetry Festival and the Burnaby Writers Society Poetry Contest.

MÉIRA COOK is completing graduate work at the University of Manitoba. Her first book of poetry, *A Fine Grammar of Bones,* was published by Turnstone Press in 1993. More recently, she has had a chapbook published by disOrientations press, entitled *The Ruby Gavotte*.

JOAN CRATE teaches English at Red Deer College. Her book of poetry, *Pale and Real Ladies: Poems for Pauline Johnson*, published by Brick Books, has just gone into its third printing. Her novel *Breathing Water* was published by NeWest Press in 1989.

KAREN DETLEFSEN has had her poems published in *blue buffalo*, *Prairie Journal of Canadian Literature*, and *Whetstone*. She is a graduate of the University of Calgary, taught English in Botswana, and is continuing her studies in philosophy at the University of Western Ontario.

PAULETTE DUBÉ was born on the prairies and will die on the prairies, with some movement in between. Her awards include the James Patrick Folinsbee Prize in English, first place in the *Edmonton Journal* 22nd Annual Literary Awards, Alberta Film and Literary Arts Grants, and the Milton Acorn Memorial People's Poetry Award. Her first book, *The House Weighs Heavy,* was published by Thistledown Press in 1992.

JENNIFER FOOTMAN lives in Brampton, Ontario, where she tries to write nearly full-time. Her poetry, fiction, and feature articles have been published in many Canadian, U.K., and U.S. magazines. She has two collections of poetry published: *Through a Stained Glass Window* (Envoi Press, 1989) and *Gathering Fuel in Vacant Lots* (HMS Press, 1992).

MARTA M. GASSLER was born and raised in Austria, and immigrated to Canada twenty years ago. Her poems have appeared in literary magazines and have been purchased by CBC Radio.

LEA HARPER is a singer and composer who has released three records, one of which was nominated for a Juno award. Her poem, "Commencement of Tai Chi," has been chosen for the *Windhorse Reader: Choice Poems of '93*.

LISA HEBDEN is a first year Visual Arts student at the University of Victoria. Her poems and paintings have been published in the *Claremont Review* and the BCETA Student Writing Journal.

DAVID HENDERSON is a poet living in Ottawa. In 1994 he won second prize in the Canadian Authors Association, Ottawa Branch, Free Verse Competition.

CORNELIA HOOGLAND has two books of poetry, *The Wire-Thin Bride* (Turnstone Press) and *Marrying the Animals* (Brick Books). Her poetry has appeared in most of the League's poetry contest anthologies and was nominated for the 1993 National Magazine Poetry Award.

SUSAN IOANNOU is a poet and writing teacher at the Rosedale Heights High School and the Ryerson Literary Society in Toronto. She founded Canada's first correspondence course for poets, the Poetry Tutorial, and is director of Wordwrights Canada editing and author services. Her book of poetry, *Clarity Between Clouds*, was published by Goose Lane Editions in 1991.

SOPHIA KASZUBA was born in Europe, grew up in Northern Ontario, and now lives in Toronto. She has published poetry in a number of magazines, including *Arc, Antigonish Review, CVII, Dandelion, Quarry, Poetry Canada,* and *Writ*.

LOIS R. KERR is a poet living in Vancouver.

CARROLL L. KLEIN is a writer and editor by trade, and a cook and traveller by nature. She is a member of the Calliope Writing Group of Kitchener-Waterloo.

LAURIE KRUK received her Ph.D. in English from the University of Western Ontario. *Theories of the World*, her first book of poetry, was published in 1992 by Netherlandic Press. She has recently accepted a full-time appointment at Nipissing University in North Bay, Ontario.

GENEVIEVE LEHR was born in Newfoundland. She received her M.A. from the University of Ottawa in 1991 and teaches Adult English as a Second Language in Prince George, British Columbia. Her songbook, *Come and I Will Sing You: A Newfoundland Songbook*, was published in 1985. Her awards include the Gregory Power Poetry Awards, first prize, 1986 and the *Tickle Ace* Poetry Awards, 3rd prize, 1993.

BARRY MACDOUGALD wrote "Olduvai Gorge" in memory of Louis and Mary Leakey. They taught us so much about ourselves.

SUE MACLEOD lives in Halifax with her ten-year-old daughter (and their dog). Her poems have appeared in journals across Canada, including *Poetry Canada*, *CVII*, *Fireweed*, and *Prism International*.

SUSAN A. MANCHESTER is an English teacher and poetry workshop co-ordinator in Toronto. Her poetry has been published in *The Georgia Review*, *Yankee*, *Negative Capability*, *TickleAce* and many other small magazines. She is the winner of a Milton Dorfman Poetry Prize and a *Poetpourri* National Contest in the U.S.

ROB MCLENNAN, on good days, claims to be the reincarnation of Richard Brautigan. He has published six chapbooks, and likes to edit things. He lives in Ottawa.

COLIN MORTON has published four books of poetry, including How To Be Born Again (Quarry), and co-produced the animated poetry film, *Primiti Too Taa*. His first novel, *Oceans Apart*, was published in 1995 by Quarry Press as part of the New Canadian Novelists Series.

LISA NACKAN was born in Johannesburg, South Africa, and is currently a Creative Writing student at York University. She dedicates her time to writing and anti-racism work. Her poems have appeared in *The African Oracle* and *Womyn's Words*.

SHARON H. NELSON'S recent books include *Family Scandals*, *Grasping Men's Metaphors*, and *The Work of Our Hands*. She served as a founding co-ordinator of the Feminist Caucus of the League of Canadian Poets.

JOHN PASS lives near Sakinaw Lake on British Columbia's sunshine coast. He and his wife run High Ground Press, which specializes in letterpress printing and publication of limited edition poetry broadsheets and chapbooks. In 1988, he won the CIVA Canadian Poetry Prize and was short-listed for the Dorothy Livesay Prize in 1991.

JULIE PAUL writes in Victoria, British Columbia, where she works as a Registered Massage Therapist. This is her first published work.

JANIS RAPOPORT is an award-winning writer whose fifth book of poetry, *After Paradise,* was published in 1995. Her recent writing is featured in *Modern Poetry in English* (Copp Clark Longman).

JOHN REIBETANZ teaches at the University of Toronto. His poems have appeared in *Canadian Literature*, *Quarry*, *Poetry* (Chicago), and *Descant*, and most recently in *The Malahat Review* and *The Paris Review*. His second collection, *Morning Watch*, was published by Véhicule Press in 1994.

ROBERT C. RUTTAN is a high-school English teacher — in theory. In fact, he is a supply teacher, living with his wife in the upper part of a barn outside of Baxter, Ontario. In 1988 and 1994 he received grants from the Ontario Arts Council Writers' Reserve Fund. This is his first publication.

MARK SINNETT moved to Canada from England in 1980, where he spent the first sixteen years of his life. He has had his poetry published widely, including appearances in *Quarry*, *The Antigonish Review*, and *Carousel*.

JANET SIMPSON-COOKE'S first book of poetry, *Future Rivers,* was published by Ragweed Press in 1987, and was on the short list for that year's Gerald Lampert Award.

EVA TIHANYI'S latest collection of poems, *Saved by the Telling*, is forthcoming from Thistledown Press in 1995. She is currently teaching part-time at Niagara College in Welland, Ontario.

BRENDA TIMMINS is a second year anthropology student at the University of Waterloo. Although she is dyslexic, she continues to be an honour student. She has been writing for two years, and is a member of the Calliope Writers Group of Kitchener-Waterloo.

JOHN UNRAU has published poems in a variety of Canadian, American, and Irish periodicals. His poems have been published in three previous anthologies of the League of Canadian Poets.

PATIENCE WHEATLEY has had two books of poetry published: *A Hinge of Spring* (Goose Lane Editions, 1986) and *Good-bye to the Sugar Refinery* (Goose Lane Editions, 1990). Her poems have appeared in *Prairie Schooner*'s Canadian Women Writers issue (Winter, 1993), *More Garden Varieties* (Aya/Mercury Press, 1989), and many other anthologies.

PATRICIA YOUNG has had four books of poetry published and has received numerous awards for her poetry. Her most recent book, *More Watery Still* (House of Anansi, 1992), was nominated for the 1992 Governor General's Award for Poetry.

Vintage 94

LEAGUE OF CANADIAN POETS

Snowy Owl After Midnight

I like to believe he waits for me
in the dark pines along the river,
eyes trained on the porchlight
of my house;
I like to believe his blood stirs
at my presence, in a way unknown
to him, but that he also understands
the heightened smell of joy and fear
my bones give off
as I shut the door behind me
and plunge into the stars.

It is so quiet at this hour,
just the two of us awake,
each hunting in his way
the small gifts of the night,
what he seeks in the long grass
and marshes, what I seek
in the soft, unpeopled silence:
at first I thought I followed him
along the dyke and through the fields,
privy to a ritual strange and
wild in its solitude;
now I'm not so sure.

For miles
he wings above my shoulder
quick and small as those moons
we watched in childhood
from the backseats of our parents' cars,
those moons that always raced us home,
that we could never lose

and when I stop, he's there,
settling on a fence-post or piling,
diving behind a clump of trees;
never a shriek from the grass
never a word from my throat;
we have circled each other's silence
this way for months.

Again, tonight, I wonder
what he would tell me if he could;
would he say the blood that calls him
to the earth is a blood
he does not understand?
Under these drumming wings I wonder
what death does he expect
my clipped, pale hands to make?

I would say to him now,
this blank page riffling in the night,
this beating heart of a snowman
extant from some boyish dream,
brother, I have stopped my ears against
the blood that calls me to the earth
but I will move here with you
in its dark and silent flowing
as long as breath is given
and your vigil burns white fire in the trees.

Reprieve For The Body

The body wants wind it can fall back on, involuntarily
hurried along a few flighty steps, arms outstretched

wants the hands of the masseuse divining
completely its faults and shudders, its taproots and aquifers.
The body wants its walking daylight, daily
bread of whole air and things seen at the right pace.

The body half-wants to carry in 21 sheets of gyproc
from the truck by itself in the rain even. It doesn't

want its bicycle, its skis, its Nautilus machine
so much as a clean dive into the lake
and coming up straight-limbed and strong with the force
of the water's counterweight on its heels, eyes opening
breaking into the bright world with a whoop.

But the body appreciates definition and discipline
tempered with wit, wants to make the unlikely serve
deservedly, likes to get lucky in the back-court, the deep corners.

I don't make an argument for the body
has no use for argument not even the flawed
patient struggle the poem has saying
what it hopes is true. The body shakes it off, phooey

like a labrador

and goes on wanting the blurred reciprocal urgency
of lovemaking at its best, the body dressed in its splendour of kisses

the brave-hearted body electric, the 20th-century body
in the earth-chair kneeling at the terminal needing its ground.

The body wants its earth

especially stumbling off the train where it's been a waiter
legs braced against the sway, tray centered in its left palm
2 days Vancouver to Winnipeg and 2 days return 10 hours later

especially deplaning at Narita it wants
no cunningly wired and padded layover pod but a loud
pebbled beach, its remembered cherry tree, sun-hot granite slab on Fuji.

The body wants to lie down on the ground and stay put
till dusk, rolling over now and then as it pleases
feeling its way, dreaming its magnificence, its breath and fingers

ruffling the wild mint, the heaped grass-clippings, the leaves'
musk under the hedges, dead-still as the neighbour victim

of knock-out-ginger crashes onto his porch
his houselights raging, or strangers

go by on the sidewalk, their voices lonely and trivial —
an aching poetry wanting the singing body
so near, forsaken, so sullen with its losses
it won't come in for calling for the longest time.

What the Dog Dreams

Sometimes we chuckle at him,
flopped out flat like a cardboard cut-out.
We could prop him up and get

dog: side view

These summer evenings
he shuns the dim and empty rooms
and sleeps in our way in the doorway,
body on the soft diningroom carpet
and head on the cool kitchen floor.

Snorts. Twitches.
Tremors here and there:
minor earthquakes. Small growls
rise in his throat. And now and then
a sound between a whimper
and the whinny of another
bent, shaped animal.

He's our child who won't grow up,
the one who'll always like our gifts
and never slam the door on us.

Listening to his deepening snores
we wonder what the dog dreams.
Is his brain encoding data
for a future generation?
and the ears will be shaped in such and such a manner
to protect them when the head sticks out the backseat window
Does he dream of how the green field looks
at 90 k per hour?

My daughter says he's dreaming
of the treat we gave him earlier.
We laughed when he took it from our hands
and skulked around a corner, as if one of us,
his hungry pack-mates, would snitch it back.

Mornings, we go to the park
and set him free to lope across the hills
and pathways, roll on his back
in the grass, and chase.
Flocks of gulls and pigeons
swarm in his wake.

Nights, he settles
and re-settles in the hollow rooms.
Faint flicks
of numbers on digital clocks.
The rise and fall of human breath.

I think he dreams of happy times,
chasing gulls and smart-assed cats,
and of moments when his nails
don't click on concrete.
I think he dreams of running on the earth
and because we're what he knows
he dreams us with him. Snout to snout,
our noses wet, paws pounding.
Dreaming us
our fur back on.

He Made Her Pregnant

She sobs. She doesn't want any more.
That big head of yours, she says to me,
the dents of the forceps still in my skull.
Perhaps, I'm his fault too. When she's angry
at me she shouts, *You'll see what its like*
to suffer when you have your own.

I try to imagine the bland voice behind
the newspaper. The man who chuckles at
Fibber McGee and Molly, and plays the music
low before going to bed at ten. I try to imagine
him pinning her, prying her legs apart with
those big raw hands, plunging her.

Once I saw him drown kittens in a bucket of water,
the kittens we'd just seen born, all black and slimy,
their eyes still milky blind. His hands pushed
down and down those little pink noses
                              hungry for air.
At night in bed, she sucks in her breath. *You're*
hurting me. I freeze, breathless at the breathing
behind the curtain strung between our rooms.
Sometimes, when she goes out, I strut in the
pubescent dark and admire my own lovely

burgeonings. Wish they were pendulous like
hers with swollen dark brown nipples she loves
to display. He hears a noise, drops his paper,
comes to the door. *What's going on in here?*
I scurry into bed. Dare him to come in.

Checking Up On Gould

His thin thin hands.

I had seen them before, but
not so still; or long enough
to really appreciate them, to
study all the joints. Find,
in other words, a dozen new reasons
for the ways they moved.

I can only imagine
the machine they must have
wheeled in to the room
for that last shot of his hands' bones:
the lengthy x-ray that showed knuckles
dancing like puppets in front of
grey walls — disjointed, a touch mad.

The room mapped out:

The Steinway   the x-ray machine
      the french sliding doors

                  & out
            to a patio
            he often walked
            . . . in soft shoes

those early footfalls
like a series of plums
dropped into sand.

It seems too technical, in the end,
to have put so cold a machine in a room
so warm, lined with paper textured as if
the skin from peaches was preserved there,
a fur peeled off slow, & arranged
into immense, subtle pattern. To say,
when the camera has hummed its way
down into silence, 'Play something then.
Play something dramatic for all the people
in the movie houses, sat upright
in the thick fluttering dark.'

Perhaps instead they had him go right in
to the hospital,
                    directed him
from behind stiff leaden curtains.

Or else these are not his hands at all,
on the film, in the dark. And those fingers
that scuttle about
                    in that grey celluloid wash
like crabs on a darkened beach,
are those of a stand-in. Maybe a woman
did this, or else just someone
the director found by chance, a man
drumming his fingers on a windowsill,
watching the clock and waiting
for a word — any word — from doctors
who have learnt some way to lean
against the air, to stand completely still
in their long ivory-white jackets.

School Children in the Kalahari

Sophie sits behind Ledulo, plaits Ledulo's hair.
And a woman stands behind them, removed,
listening to a language she has not
learned, loves only for its strangeness, its complete openness
to meaning. She thinks *I can dream these words into anything
I want: a conversation of truths
neither doubts, a revelation of love.*

Sophie draws a thin blue thread from the broken
part of Ledulo's sweater, knots a row of hair, begins a new
one. What the woman really wants is a way of explaining
the distance she has travelled to the man
she left behind. She wants to find
the word that will make him
want more than anything to unfurl
his fingers from around her.

She knows the word
is not in this language. It is unspeakable. She believes
she might find it in the patterns of holy
bones strewn to tell the faith
healer the cure to sickness. Perhaps it is hidden
in the curved ridges of sand which speak
of the journeys of mambas.
How can she write this — a word that isn't — in a letter
to a man who has a name for everything. Even as this phantom
word skitters along the edges of her understanding,
she understands clearly the man
will define it immediately.

bush-fever   he will call it   *madness*

Sophie plaits and plaits, reins
each wild strand in, tames, contains
and behind them a woman is dying more slowly than any
eye could see, something even larger than a desert
submerging her. No word, no word
at all could ever make it past the fist
tightening at her throat.

Sophie lays her cheek on Ledulo's spine
between the two sharp blades
of her shoulders. She curls her long and gentle
arms around her friend. Somewhere in the shadows
of that sheltering is the thing
Ledulo cannot see. A tiny hole growing over
the back part, the dark part
of her own heart.

Passport

I sleep in a hot country,
trace borders with my tongue,
settle in the soil creviced
between your limbs.

The land I love is foreign.
I linger in orchards of figs,
dates, carob. You pick each fruit
for me, offer them with words
I can't understand spoken
in a familiar voice.
    khudi, habibti
Beneath my lips your heart
explodes, explodes, explodes.

We lie in a strange bed.
Your father's house has no roof
and I search the eastern sky
for an unshattered star to feed you,
a beacon to hold in your throat
instead of the word "good-night."

Your lids click shut and a dark continent
falls between us.

Oh, but I own a passport to your heart.
I travel your distance,
swim with you in the Mediterranean,
play Hearts in a bombed-out basement in Beirut.

I lose my way

on roads of winding veins
stumble upon a trail
of cigarette burns partially obscured
in a forest of black hair.
Now I know

where to find all your scars.
I give them names and causes:
a chance fall while stealing almonds,
a childhood fight, barbed wire,
half-hearted torture.
They are the roadblocks to my dreams,
the first indication of nightmare
you will not discuss you

refuse to heal
refuse to mourn

I silently draw you into my landscape,
wash your wounds in cool, clean daylight.

Srebrenica Suite

1. Bombed

In the blown-out wall
midnight's dragonflies

rise with sparks
to blacken the moon.

2. To a Bride of War

I lay the lilies of hate, my love,
along your bloodied hair.
From twisted foot and crumpled dress
the blue bruise crawling up your cheek
collapses a last breath.
May long white petals perfume your death.

Rubble is your marriage bed.
Blackened beams let in the sky.
Frost fills an emptied shoe.

Sleep quiet
though new thunder splits
this battered rock, and air bursts red.

I lay these lilies by your head
to wed you with old earth.

3. The Abandoned Hospital

Bone-withered
their eyes are like peeled eggs
turning black, and back
inside half-emptied skulls.

Fingers, red lumps puffed with cold,
cannot hold even tatters
over transparent skin.

Pieces of selves, not people,
their fireworked nerves shudder.
Above, the fractured moon
dangles its sparking cord.

4. Survivor

Each night,
a black-scarved woman
squats by the riverbank.

Her small net
splashes and crawls
— a boot? a bone?

Behind,
barbed wire
catches the moon.

5. After the Raid

No clear deep pool
where pebbles shiver
but a looking glass steamed over

her face floats up nothing.

6. Torturer

We expect a face
that could splinter mirrors:
nose, a long interrogation point,
eyes, sharpened skewers,
mouth, a red sneer,

but after shrieks' steel in the bone,
not his casual turning away,
the half-hidden yawn.

JENNIFER CHEW

tradition

my brother saw, he saw
a dead baby girl
floating down the river
the cold yellow river
a small pale dead baby
floating down the river

small because she was newborn
pale because she was dead
dead because she was not a boy

she was floating down the river
and farmers walked along
the riverside, talking
their feet leaving shallow holes
in the soft earth
their feet dislodging stones
that fell into the river
they walked along the riverside
she floated down the river
my brother stopped
as she floated down
and floated down further

stopped because she was floating
stopped because he was a foreigner
stopped because he didn't understand

tradition

Soldiers

I saw them on the six o'clock news
migrate
  from Bosnia to Israel
  from cries of war to cries of help
until there is a blending
of Intifada and Serbs
a fusion of freedom fighters and enemy forces
  similar faces
  only channels apart
armed with rocks with leftover weapons
the surplus of conflicts in pause.

The soldier looks behind
chest expanding focus narrow
rifle swung low on a strong back
the stance of all warriors
the erotic stance of soldiering
the knees bend as the weapons rise.

This is the seduction
  of boys who join
  the boys who bond to these men
in the homo-erotic part of war
and keeps them there
enlisted in the stranglehold of similar men
  with the same attachment
  to the same piece of ground.

Again on the nine o'clock news
scenes of pre-orgasmic soldiers
raising guns arms taut legs apart
ready for the moment when they will prove
  some thing
to a constantly watching world.

nathan phillips square

the reflection of downtown toronto city blocks
filters into the pond at my feet
fountains charge into the sky
black   white   gray shadows   gallop across the water
zebra manes ripple in my mind

blue laps the edges
azure of africa
so bright i want to touch the outline   steal a piece
hide it in my pocket
until the next downcast day

i sit under this maple
a fallen leaf in my lap
in the kruger park zebras hide below umbrella trees
scatter through grasses
keep open watchful eyes

when i see a zebra hide
draped over a floor
i cannot walk over it
but in this downtown pond
i wish i could walk on water

feel zebra stampede
forever untamed
and this kaleidoscope of stripes
will spill no blood
between black and white

———

(Kruger Park — a nature conservation park in South Africa)

Woman on Her Way to Market

No matter what negotiators said
It cost her life to walk across a street —
A sniper put a bullet through her head.

She began to cross then crossed herself instead.
An inky pool of blood grew around her feet
No matter what negotiators said

Around a table with the best intent.
She wondered what her family could eat
Then a sniper put a bullet though her head.

Shells flew over where she lay and bled
Her last words out into the empty street.
No matter what negotiators said

No time was given to remove the dead.
None claim victory, none admit defeat.
A sniper put a bullet through her head

Then went home to supper, children, wife and bed
To lose her memory in a dreamless sleep.
No matter what negotiators said
A sniper put a bullet through her head.

midnight mass

the priest and his angels appear in smoke
the church coughs through handkerchiefs and hands
the murmuring candles
smell of waxed benches
make my eyes heavy and turn my bones to sand

i cuddle against my mother
her lavender coat with fur cuffs
tickles my nose but i play with buttons
while Mme Sabourin slumps down ahead of us
black hair disappearing
under the weight of a full fur coat

Maman clucks her tongue
"I s'pose he thought he was doing her a favor"
the priest drones on
as three men pull and push the fur coat towards the door

i thing it would be better if they fixed Mme's shoe
it hangs crazy from her toes
like it is trying to run away

Glass Walls

Year after year the robin built her nest
beside the silvery window
day after day she sat on a branch
of the prickly thorn
    her cocky eye lured
    by the bright shine of lamps
    the warm glow of brass and teak
    a bowl of red apples

time after time she flew from her branch
expecting to enter
time after time with a definite thud
she spiralled to the ground

    crazy robin is back
    the children said
    she'll never learn

DAVID W. HENDERSON

Burn-Out

In a lab long ago, he remembers
photos of a light bulb
with a bullet rifling through it.
what most impressed him, the frames
he best recalls, were the ones
where the bullet had come
and gone, yet still the light bulb
held together. Now,

he's become that light bulb, still
retaining his shape, still pretending
nothing's wrong — but fissured,
in danger of losing his composure.

Outside his office, July melts
the asphalt, while he sits
glassed-in, frozen before his screen.
So much he'd like to do —
delete botched files, reconfigure
memory, adopt simpler protocols —
but he's paralyzed
by the void beneath the cursor,

by the in-basket
with its eruption of documents
spilling over the desk,
by the miscarriage of ideas,
by the rumours circulating
endlessly from office to office,
along with the odours
of hair spray, coffee,
flatulence and disinfectant.

Tragedy's too big a word
for it, but the fact is
he dares not move,
for, if he does, he'll be
carried to the frames beyond,
where the fissures grow
and catenate until
the light bulb flies apart.

The Meditative Prayer
of the Man in Love
With Sensation

early december:a cool morning & he pulls his dark car to a remote
roadside between snow spotted hills:farmland around nodding
fenceposts the wire between same grey as the surrounding sky &
wavering post to post desperate to get there by all routes possible
                                        steps from his car   gazes
across fog & rough brown fields & washed lines of trees at their
borders:pulls slowly on the cool air & flat colours around him:this
precious filling of eyes & lungs:breeze pushed his thinning brown
hair:he listens
                    to rumours playing through his head:of faith
's delicacy:that it might be lost: the cold air again in his lungs:its
spreading like arms
                            outstretched inside his chest:the
smell of cool wet conifers:texture of the field:damp&brown&cold:flat
brown&grey&cold with its arms outstretched inside him:rumours of
delicacy persist:
                        he steps into the road:the
sound of his footsteps:spotted grey horse hardly visible:the wind
adjusts his hair:
                        he stretches arms
akimbo:sucks in enough air for a cyclone:to last as much of his
remaining life as it is needed to

Discordant Season

In the beginning of this dangerous age
where my youth has just toppled
and I am dizzy with the sudden glory
and the sudden descent
I see how the harsh rush of the river
is tender to rocks
how fallen trees yield magnificently
to forest floor
how my bones and skin relinquish
a name
how I have come a twisted way
to sing my song

our middle-aged hearts
now a ridge of downed trees
where desire menaces
the flame of self
And will you once alone
mourn so the mourning
is more lovely
than the mornings
when our first movement
is to touch?

yet the heart
always the heart intends love
my hand, a garland of flowers
is outstretched
though the line of youth is crossed
though you live in many rooms
without me
our one verse, age-old
and drumming
to a discordant season.

The House of Lorca

I visit the House of Lorca up in heaven
in the place of the Christians who live
side by side with the Moors and Gypsies.
Lorca fills the sky with his voice of the night.
It is dusk and the water in the fountain is falling
slowly in the darkening square.
Lorca's music is a green circle
where bougainvillea falls,
as his music falls, over and over again,
down the slow curves in the dark, the way
the Madonna is worshipped behind the green Christ
with her blue cloak like a sheet of water in sunlight,
like a mirror into which birds look when they sing.
The poem of Lorca is singing with them
of the glory heaven is, when we open,
as he can open, his eyes in the light
and look out of the darkness and see,
God and Christ, and Mary
who is always with him
with her hand in his arm, speaking
of the resurrection of the body,
of the body flared into light like a word.

Artist

this artist has
a landscape
always in his head

we go willingly
into every field
where he calls us

a night darker than memory
holds us
the moonrise
lights our faces
we hear the voices
of eternity

we hear our hearts' thunder
we welcome new life

his canvas is the home
we've always wanted
but could never create
it is the place that
makes us his

makes us real

there is only clear
white space to become
what we will

a voice beyond the wilderness
that reaches us at night

pulls us into the dark

into the center of stars
there is a heart beating
a light brighter than any sun

we are not afraid

we listen to the music
of star points
and recognize our own voices
home is any sky over us

home is the life he gives
any landscape

home becomes us
frees us
to become the image
he makes
makes us whole
there are no missing parts
white space to be filled

to become

what we will

The Call

1

Was that You? A ripple, arrowing through
the rows of barley, making no more noise
than the wind does when it strokes their tassels.
A call, but in the kind of sign language

that shyness and a mind for teasing would
conspire to shape, a mute challenge you knew
I'd be too slow to pick up. To follow
across the field at dusk, leap the tangled

masses of deadfall bordering the pines,
and zigzag through the undergrowth without
breaking an ankle or heading into
a tree: that was your specialty, not mine.

2

I marvel at Nature's reckless spending,
how she throws lives around like small change: each
rabbit the foxes get to, each chipmunk
frozen with tiny feet stretched out, unique

as the dapple on each leaf as leaves drop
by the millions. And you, my elusive
whitetail, the pattern of extravagance
sprouting from your head afresh each summer,

fast-growing branchwork that outpaced the trees
only to be cast off when the snows came:
was your airy leap also a spendthrift's toss,
or a headlong break to throw off gravity?

3

Living in the country is like standing
under a shining cascade of shed things,
a flotsam of short lives spilling over
the unmoving edge. So I should have guessed,

on skis, doing my level best to catch
what I remembered of your grace of stride,
that the bare stalk tipped over in the field
was no small tree. Though the wolves pared your bones

to match the antler that you hadn't cast,
none of the knobby awkwardness of bones
hampered in its branching flow, a silk-gloved hand
tracing one last leap, daring me to follow.

Solar Aspects

The sun is a medallion pinned on a blue cloth,
a crown forged through a harvest of heat, a shield
against perpetual dark. The sun is an apple, an apricot,
a peach, a red plum. It's an orange tomato ripening
on a summer vine. The sun is a flower always in bloom
a single pea in a pod, a cheese bagel, a pancake
on a cosmic plate cooking away in an alchemical kitchen
designed by physicist gourmets. The sun is dessert,
a multi-layered cake of hydrogen and helium, swirled
with scarlet plume icing, accented by burnt-out candles
of stellar ash. Post dessert it's a bright candy looping
along the throat, spiciest against tongue and teeth.
As an eye the sun travels just under Ra's forehead
across the sky in a boat, attended by hawks, scarabs
and rams' horns while vulture wings beat.
The sun is a cell, a spore, a seed, a knot of light
we hope will keep turning. The sun is the rim
of a well, a bucket of wishes, a newly formed stone
shot through Apollo's bow in his pursuit of Niobe.
The sun is music, inspiration and peace, a disc
radiant with prophecy, a gambling chip or coin,
a record we've all forgotten. The sun is a baseball
pitched into the galaxy, a button that dresses
the afternoon, a lamp we use but can't turn off or on.
Under its honeycomb of light Atlas sweats,
lifting the earth on naked shoulders, suspended forever
at the border of night and day. The sun is rouge
on the face of the sky, a mouth feasting on atoms.
The sun marks the end of a sentence with blood,
seals the red roof of tomorrow. The sun is a violet wound,
a tarnished gong that cannot drown.

Olduvai Gorge

And you believe in the lie that we escaped Olduvai!
Why then do my creaking old bones still struggle to scrape this soil?
Why am I tracing my way through this gorge still?
Why am I holding my belly, collecting beer bottles, urine samples,
Looking for evidence of life?

Was this a man?

This his wife?

Did all life really begin here?

How long did these bones struggle to climb out?

Using a teaspoon, I dig deeply into the fruit of human evolution.
I rut about in roots searching for antecedents,
Scooping at seed that flowed long ago in different flowers,
How different those flowers, those seeds, that life.

The DNA pours from lost bones like bitter summer forecasts of what the
    weather will be like
As I journey back down the path of my own genes, and I find a Wasoo.

"Oh Wasoo! What a big nose you had! And what big eyes. And what sharp
    teeth!
Could you smell me coming to visit this lofty perch, this pit,
This high-flown refuse mine of who was who in history?
These bones that I have found, are they yours or did they come from a baboon?
Did the baboon share a meal with you, an antecedent, a mirror,
Or did you look down upon the baboon as some now do on you?
Oh, how immortally alike you and the baboon have become with the passing of
    years!

"Did you kill for pleasure, or for survival?
Did you see stars, or did you lack the time? The urge? The sense to look up?
Did you love then only for companionship or for keeping the stars alive?
How old were you, Wasoo when you first learned to speak, read, create
    pictures, imagine?
How deep was your knowledge? How high your gods?
What godlike potential seeped into these bones as you crept through ooze in
    marshes
That dampened your bottom like gentle watering a clay pot?
How careful was your cleansing? How clever the covering of your offerings to
    nature?
In my hand I hold shared gifts — your bones and your droppings equally
    golden.

"Learn from me old bones, dry dust. Learn from me.
Trace your lips across the rim of this glass.
Drink your fill of this cup though it hold nothing but dust; drink your fill of
    dust!
A camel may wander but a week without water through the heat of life,
But you have drifted waterless for millions of years through this lifeless gorge.
Look with wonder then upon this journey that brought you to me.

"And dance with me then if you will. You shall lead. I shall follow.
Shall it be slow steps, or perhaps a tango?
Don't you know anything that doesn't have a drum stuck deep within the beat
    of it somewhere
Beating away as if without drums there would be no pulse?
What need have you of pulse? For two million years, you danced the dance
    that needs no pulse.
Our dance will be a close one, then. The tapping of my teaspoon will be our
    drums.

―――――――――――――――――――――――――――

"Some dance partner you are! You let your hair grow, your nails, your beard,
Never once cleaned your ears, brushed your teeth.
Took sunbaths under a G star not knowing language when you heard it,
Trampled about like a weed in your own garden
And became a man when men were animals,
And never once denied it — in the denying the difference.

"You were never the caretaker of your own droppings.
The first of the modern scholars, you scraped out a living
And dropped your thoughts, never caring where they fell.
The droppings, too, evolved. They moved through history as you did, lock step
— A million years to invent the wheel,
— Countless thousands more clothes, reasoning, manners.

"Oh how I would love to have been with you when you first controlled fire!
It was then that you dropped into low gear and began a running crawl up the
wall of history.
Who was there then to dare tamp you back down into the pipe?
You looked about in the ooze from which you first drew breath and blamed the
    gods.

"Fools!

"We were the only god that mattered — Us, We — the fruit of the first flesh
    to imagine gods.
Oh how dusty your ideas have become!
Lost in your Christmasses like cattle on the grassy knoll of time
You continually edged closer to the brink of this gorge that holds us all.
How tuned were your voices to the sounds that came from an historical
    snowdrift
No plow could ever sweep away?
Did your upright feet in their new shoes feel the pinch of this snow?
Did your fingers freeze and your hands tremble as your arms made welcoming
    gestures
To bellies ripe with this seed fresh from your God?

"You could never imagine a smattering of generations hence how powerful you
    would become.
We piled seed on your dust so high. We buried you deep,
So deep you will never recover from the sleep that stills you and anchors you
    like a chain
To the ooze that sifts through a gorge that you could not see, could not feel,
    could not name."

Tortoise

"from Old French tortue (Latin tortus twisted), from Medieval Latin tortuca, from Late Latin tartarucha coming from Tartarus, from Greek tartaroukhos; referring to the belief that the tortoise originated in the underworld"
— Collins English Dictionary

metamorphosis
of rock and tree root,
you mirage,
breathed into living mystery
resting beneath the guard rail
between creek and roadside,
lower world and upper,
all twelve inches of you
immobilized in world-weariness — right there,
in the current moments,
of gravel-spitting cars and buzzing cyclists:
your eternity

But I must stop, and look
into unblinking elephantine eyes
and prudish mouth. Center of human curiosity
the tortoise is unmoved, unmoving and unrevealing
half-buried by its Sisyphean burden
of basaltic shell-rock
cryptically carved
by evolution's knife.

Tortoise,
you remind us of the torturous path
we've taken
up to these iron roads,
forsaking the buggy coolness and mud below
for the dangerous dust we glory in.

Silent witness,
cathedral shell a testament
to your weight of judgment,
taloned feet scoring the dirt
with casual force,
your delicate snake's neck
and mute beak refuse to make
even the slightest sign
of a sign
that we share your world.

In our age of speed,
you wait with the intensity
of an inferno saint.

Give us knowledge, Saint
of your inarticulate weight.

Stones

stones settle into earth
like cats in winter
dissolve into the soft shapes of rooms

stones submit to their fates
ease their roots down and down
to the warmed earthy dark

stones keep their quiet history
years pass   time beyond counting
and the stars still wander   universal vagrants
the breath of humanity blows and is silenced
the earth opens and closes
catastrophe and salvation stalk the hills

where stones live   windworn   turned to the sky
breathing in unison   edging into circles
where the brown grass sways and sways
heedless of the stone dance   the old song

Buffalo Hills

humps   in the hollows wooly
patches of brown shrub   lean flanks
of yellow fescue grass   buffalo

turned hills   bare hills a herd
of buffalo   a herd of heaving slopes
wind in the furry tussocks   rippling

the solitary bull   erratic remnant of
a glacier   sun warm on ridge of lowered
neck   wide wet nose is sniffing

a group of boulders   rising shoulders
from the ground   rock power   dense
and slow   unleashed   curved horns

a tearing front   a rushing crushing mass
of legs   hooves spraying clumps of trampled
earth   a rumbling   clouds of dust

hills   sunning   Indian summer   lazy
whip of tails   shape of land   a buffalo
resting   stretching autumn hills

Wanuskewin
(Cree for Seeking Peace of Mind) Heritage Park,
Near Saskatoon

A woman watches a child trying to climb up the rough face of the cliff at Newo Asiniack Jump. The woman's skin tightens onto her bones; she holds a sick fascination with the very idea of a buffalo jump and hates herself for it. She reads a sign set into a stone post beside her. It states that she is standing on bone beds and the sign itself and the funding for the inspection spot have been provided by Morgan Fibrocarbons Ltd. For two thousand years the buffalo have been driven off the cliff above her and the maimed have been killed and their flesh, hides, horns, teeth and hooves been used. The women of the tribe even found a purpose for the foetus of any dead cow. They made it into a bag for carrying water. The bones of the buffalo were left season by season, fall and spring, to form these bone beds. There is no indication she is standing on layer upon layer of bone. A loud snap makes her look again at the child who has just broken a sapling. The child's father examines the damage and gathers a handful of twigs, pulls some long grass and splints the sapling with twigs and grass. The child takes his father's hand. Father and mother nod fondly at each other over their son's head. It's as if they agree between themselves that, yes, everything can be mended. The family don't seem in any hurry to leave the bone beds. The watching woman walks past them quickly and as she does so, she gets a whiff of heavy, heady perfume. Jasmine. Joy. Her mother used to wear Joy. And also the smell of tobacco. One of the family smokes. She climbs the path up out of the bone bed.

Like Rain

                The landscape
does not vindicate our likeness
five figures poise gingerly
on the edge of water.
Or take the word *mouth*
round as a vowel.

So I have come to this place
from so far away, a green parabola
fine rain sieved through skin
it is no longer possible to write
love poems or say *here I am*, here
at the day's
damp hinge, say it say
mouth.

A hundred words for green
in this damp language, enunciation
of tendril & leaf, here
at the dull syntax of rock
and throat, nothing to recall
the dead unless memory grows
purple and emphatic, splits rock

As for the deer that crossed
our path that day the road
going on without us, they have already
passed out of the present tense. I saw
two deer she says (all day rain falls
like rain) falls here and here

This is a love poem perhaps the last one
I will ever write because of this business
with deer, words turned fossil
in the lining of mouth before we can
say flicker.

Woke up this morning, imprint
of hoof on her cheek.

Calibrations

"let it not be said of me and of that which I have done he hath done deeds against that which is very right and true . . . let me have joy of heart at the weighing of words"
        — The Egyptian Book of the Dead

Your hands rest in mine
light as the feather of truth
I weigh my heart

> *my heart has been a Minotaur*
> *distracted by hot blood*
> *dark enclosed systems*
> *engorged, mindless*
> *it has eaten flesh and been consumed*

It has not led me here often

> *my heart has been a feather*
> *full of light and sky*
> *a bellows fanning air*
> *into starving lungs*

It has flown from you

> *my heart has been a drill sergeant*
> *sunk low in my chest*

I have run from you with wooden feet

Now, my hands are pilgrims
holding yours, fragile as burnt wicks,
like a prayer between them.

Helpless as a newborn
you flailed against confines,
your life shrunken to the size of this room
you still grasped at its hem
pulled it to your lips.

Your hands, bouquets of bruises,
are still now,
like that Nigerian bird I heard of,
when captive it lies unmoving
the last notes of its song so high
only children can hear.

You listen, intent,
to some internal orchestra
draining in flood

> *nights, you dream of dancing so fast*
> *you leave your wheelchair far behind*
> *feet skimming surface*
> *like birds on watery take off*
> *you dream, tingling skin*
> *a birth of feathers*

scientists spend their lives calibrating
the exact mass of a kilogram
build vaults and towers to guard its sanctity.
They do not understand
the relativity of weight.

On this threshold
we defy gravity.
Hands, so heavy I can barely lift them
aspire, become one with the light
that   falls and flies
in the breath of the
room   that slows and swells
          stretching to comprehend more
the window,
                    a widening eye of the sky.

All the weight of your life is nothing
to this song of hands
light as feathers
lifting to their highest notes.

Young Eagle On A Piling

We had thought to drift so far
meant no witness but the wild sea
and the last glazed gape
of dying salmon slicked
in their own blood at our feet;
we had thought to feel our bones
pull anchor from our flesh
as shore and safety fell away
meant an isolation known
perhaps to saint and sacrifice
but not to common men:
black clouds scraped across the sky
like stone-lids shut on sepulchres
behind which a few stars in
their pale youth stared down
pitiless. Yet we could not accept
the casual coming of the night,
how it deepened so slowly
like the blush on a grape,
how it swept over the waters
in a silent tide, dragging
its corkline of distant worlds,
its giant ghostly buoy;
we could not believe in death
of such a soft arrival

Until at the river's final marker,
a decayed piling looming just beyond
our bow, twenty feet high, like
a scorched stake kindled by
the flesh of suns, a fragment
of a Roman cross dredged up
by the current,

we felt the hour's essential hunger
pierce our skin, we felt
for the first time
our slicked hearts thrashing
in our hands: there,
calmly perched against the wind,
his feathers ruffled like the water's surface,
a young eagle looked beyond our selves
to the darker simpler facts
of fear, and what they meant
to his survival. For only a second
out of the gloom, we met
his steady yellow gaze, beacon
to a shore we had no wish
to touch, and then, as quick,
the night consumed the piling
and its patient guest

Later, the net picked up at last,
the still catch gasping in the stern,
we trained a spotlight on his perch
but he had gone,
dark ash of the day's staked sun
scattered in the storm,
raised anchor of the seeking blood
dragged across the stars,
black soul, pure need,
the truth our pretty lives
had drifted from

RHONDA BRUCHANSKI

trespasses and words of the cageling

there were seven million others like you
who used to sleep on beds of earth
alongside callalou leaves   and
sagacious grey stone which slept also

(this was a time when rain was bloodless   and man was human)

i would tell you the future has not happened   but
this would be a lie   and there is no fooling you
already   disease has burrowed its way into your skin
and you have learned to smell hunger from miles

from this   you must resign:
a land dressed with hordes of flayed creatures   and
the cankered bellies of their children conceived in cages
at gunpoint   or a knife's edge perhaps   though always
beneath something   part murderer   part god

this death of yours will be thoughtless
an insect's death
like changing a channel   merely
you think you are going home

of life   you've understood nothing
not the dreams that come to you in sleep
nothing   of those shapeless moments
during which your instinct holds purpose
and a large   blue sky exists

you know agony   loneliness   and fear
you know pain   you know you don't belong here
that there are others
because you feel a part of something   what?

me?

i look at you and i wonder where the hate is

65

at most   you've been my sacrifice
killed by the inch in science's name
this   or otherwise
the shadow of a shade   significant as crumbs

believe me   i want this to end
but each time my lips open
i taste you   then swallow my words

while your pace grows redolent of insanity
i am held captive by luxury

it is true   that in darkness i hear you   the animals
say to me   it is out of fear that we run
we run because we are chased

and the birds ask   why do you never sing to me?

and cats   the cagelings who cannot cry
who can't scream   why?   say to me
i was not born for this
i am here to give life   and
love   not blood

and so   wakeful   i avoid mirrors
this is difficult   even more
to look inside and ask

what is nature when the human eye looks at a tree and
sees a home   when the value of the elephant's long   wise life
is measured by his tusk?

and what is human
when the eye of the tree looks back at me
ax-shaped   and slaughterous
when the lion sees through bars   that i am a key?

Prairie Storm

(for and with L.L.M.)

suddenly awake
and frantic till I feel
his soft breath on my cheek
I look up from the child and see
distant lightning finger our fields

black stillness
then the monster crawls howling
at us again over the parched dirt
frenzied heart pounding harder, faster
arteries boiling
spewing scarlet all around

pillows tight
against the quivering panes;
one cracks
as hail like a trainload of gravel
thunders through the thunder overhead

3 a.m.
exhausted sleep
in the dripping kitchen
the child snug in a drawer under the table

in morning twilight
stumbling through ruin
the shed blown away
I find our turkey
huddled in a drift of hailstones

not a feather on her back:
her twelve poults safe
under wings and warm belly

Father

on the road to Frankfurt
July of fifty eight
rounding a bend toward
a red-bricked German town
you suddenly stopped the car
ignoring mother's protests
and as the five of us watched in amazement
climbed in your immaculate black suit
through a barbed-wire fence
and jogged through swath and stubble
toward three people working in a field

my window was rolled down
and from a hundred yards
I watched negotiations;
heard high-pitched protests,
laughter, and then saw you
strip off jacket, tie,
hand them to an old blue-kerchiefed woman
and taking her triple-tined pitchfork
join the other two at work

for half an hour on the road to Frankfurt
we sat and watched you stooking grain
in perfect harmony with your co-workers,
the only incongruities
your shirt of gleaming white,
the woman standing motionless like Jeeves,
your jacket folded neatly on her arm

you were on your way to give a paper
at the Max-Planck-Institute
on monosomic chromosomal substitution:
a scientist merely

but when you strode back to the car
brushing chaff and sunlight from your hair
you were to me at pimply seventeen
Odysseus come to claim his kingdom back

"Just the way we did it
at Charlie Comerford's in the thirties"
was all you said:
I think that was
the clearest sight I ever got of you.

Black Cat

(on my son's wedding night)

Tonight
Curled up on his bed,
You wait for his return,
Not knowing yet
That he will not come.

Black Cat
With the white nose and feet
A little stiff in the joints
No longer wanting to chase birds
Or play with the other cats
In the garden
Your black as black
And your white as white
As the day
He saw you being born
Choosing you for his own
And naming you "HERO"

For sixteen years
You have slept
In the crook of his knees
And in the circle of his arms
Taking his warmth
And giving your warmth to him
Consoling him in his griefs
And receiving his joys,
Always at night
Waiting
Patiently
For your summit of pleasure.

Tonight,
Curled up on his bed
Expectantly
Trustingly
You wait
For his familiar chatter
For the blare of his radio
For his nightly blitz
of untidiness.

You do not know
That he was married today
You did not see the light on his face
As he waited at the altar
For the white-bright girl.

You do not know yet
That he will not come tonight
Or tomorrow night
Or ever again
To sleep
Here in this bed.

Exchanges

We started by talking about lovers,
the can't-live-with-or-without-them scenes,
the irresistible lure of sex

By the third drink we were into families,
their blatant omnipotence,
haunting contradictions

We told of our mothers, yours
dead when you were twelve, mine
out of touch for years,
how they lived on in us
like persistent fairytale queens
necessary to the story

They were easy,
these exchanges of our female selves,
motherless, yearning;
and I've since pictured you often, like me
bent over your sleeping children
as they dream their hags and witches,
sheep in wolves' clothing

Sometimes they smile,
and we know that in *those* dreams
we are kind and soft-voiced,
the givers of music

I'm thinking of you again tonight,
imagine that provinces away
you're walking along the South Saskatchewan River
looking up, as I am,
at our shared moonlight
while our mothers speak in us
(uncanny ventriloquism),
their young selves almost singing,
audible

Editorial Remarks

1

Tenderness is not
a quality of art,
and it takes a brutal heart
to construct a poem,
toughness to cut away
its excess parts.

I'm a tailor's daughter,
watched from my cradle
material being cut,
heard the sound of the shears
from my childhood sleep.

My whole family
worked in shmattahs;
I come by my skills
honestly,
have less trouble than most
with those brutalities.

And I don't remember tenderness,
not even when my father felt
the finest cloth in his hands,
the smoothest silks,
just the necessity
to cut and shape it;
the necessity
to make a living;
no attachments
to materials.

2

You admire elegance, the craft
that makes us quiet, restrained,
against the force of pain;
rage reined in; tenderness invisible,
the thread in the seams.

3

Cloth is valued
for the tightness of its weave,
its weight, the difficulty
with which it's made.
And craft is judged
by how invisible it is.

There is no
visible expression
of tenderness
without the expectation
of encumbrances,
no thread so strong
it will not snap if overstretched,
no thread so fine or delicate
it will not catch and snarl
if pulled too fast.

Why are we shamed
by the logistics of craft,
as if clean edges and invisible seams
were a denial of love?

Why are we shamed by need,
who are not shamed to witness
every form of greed?

Tantrum

Moments we've spent alone
could fill one hand.
The most recent passed
by the ocean on a bad day;
my blood was full of storm.

No one has ever understood
this weather, father,
you are not alone.
Something crests inside,
long swells that build
up and crash at last

and fall, its wash legend
across the wetlands,
the salty random
feel of it, an undertow
not giving up the dead,
a boy's small body,

my rage, back arched
against the dank
slippery change-room floor,
legs kicking, holes
torn out of a steamy
silence of naked
men before their rotten
wooden lockers, eyes
averted, the amazement

you hurled afterward into
my mother's eyes, the hushed
accusations you were forced
up against, as she turned away.
He's my son!   You let her
blame you for everything.
I was two years old,

loved the warm embrace
of lulling waters __
leave me be! —
knowing nothing of what could
and could not be healed.
By then you knew,
knew every aching curve
beyond the viewpoint,

descending Sulphur Mountain
from the Upper Hot Springs,
1959, our cold lunch
eaten in a shelter
by some sluggish river,
the corpse-like current
dancing in the drizzle's
somnambulant tracer fire.

You kept your distance,
named it loyalty.
Loyalty the only stone
left for your defence
sinking beyond reach

through the algae-mired
mirror of an untroubled
surface, stillness
around which something
living was firmly tied.

the woman that i wrote of yesterday

is you.   watching
the sky clear her throat

of smoke   a rainbow
stroke of grey

on black stars, arcing
up from florence street,

a house on fire
/the night alive w/ bright lights

& fire trucks   a circus crowd
of performing hands & the gathered cold
/where the ash fell like butterflies

or the orange light of fireflies
                              turning in space
& then to black out, touching snow,
the woman that i wrote of,

condemning poems
to imperfect memory   the finest lines,

always, the ones composed
in the midst of morning showers, on

long hot walks in the stale air, or watching
house fires in the dead of night,
                              the wind chill
too much to speak of

the outline of your cool
white skin   my poor feet
freezing in the dense fog

the whole street blotted out by smoke
my boots, stepping lightly
in the fresh hydrant runoff,

a river encased in ice.

A dream of You

Sometimes I piece together
the terrible sadness of your face,
I piece together the way words
begin the etymology of your presence . . .

Sometimes I reconstruct the dream
and find that I am leaning on a fence
surrounded by horses. The language
you learn also leans forward, connects
the dots, makes the horse gallop, the
sky fall, makes the horse look inside
your hands for the dream's dark inventor.

Hard

(for Tenille)

The first of your 16th birthday parties
is held in the handicapped bathroom 9am
where you meet your friends between/during
boring (i.e. most) classes. Four girls
at the *mirror mirror* checking the latest
news while complaining about/
while running fingers through/
their hair.

Shalene's pan of blonde brownies shared
seated cross-legged on the floor at your lockers
where everybody (meaning the boys) will notice
will beg. Between mouthfuls will tell you
that getting your learner's a snap, you'll see.

After swimming practice, in the change
room damp from 20 hot showers
a Costco cake big as a mountain
a bush fire of candles
I can't see
not from here
not this far

I think of Blue Lady
widow's walk the tiny pacing
balconies at the uppermost reaches
of east coast houses on their tip-toes with wanting
their loved ones, missed, far out
at sea, in fishing boats, in storms
thought drowned

my girl my Blue Lady
keep your light on
I'm rowing

Coming Back

(To my adopted mother)

Your teeth are grinding in sleep
the anger you try to keep from him
In the spare room
your mouth's drawn thin as a waning moon
a moon once able to reflect the whole world
in a pool of light, a wide grin
Now night follows a thread of saliva
to a glint of tarnished pearl
and the sky shuts like a clam around your dreams

Your teeth loosen as he dismantles
the bone china figures
their perfect hands
the folded petals of white carnations
their breathing, the sound of cracked bells
or a child's pure protest

What happened to the children
muffled in their fluffy packages?
You never should have unwrapped them
screaming red like overripe tomatoes
something he could stick a finger in
to see what squirted blood, semen, tears
You knew how he loved his hooks and lures
invisible line and sinkers
prized the cold catch

In the master bedroom
dead drunk
with a lifesize blow-up doll
he's plotting the next attack on your flesh
the one the doctors will call cancer
when you relinquish each vessel
used to hold shame
the parts destroyed by brutality and neglect —
bladder, womb, vagina
and try to face God
in the neutral scrutiny of a surgical lamp

Your children are coming back from the edge
tired of the hunger strike
tired of the sun shredded through chicken wire
tired of drugs in a dixie cup
They're taking him to Drag Lake
to watch his eyes sink like two fat olives
into the last martini

Set one less place at the table
without your heart leaping onto the plate
Boil the kettle and wait
for the tea leaves to find him
gasping for air
between your cupped hands

What's left of you
is meant for happiness

Corned Beef Specials

When we make love
I think of my mother cooking
Corned Beef Specials
in her checkered sweater
stained with finger paint
watermelon marker
and tears.

I think of her standing there
holding her knife,
slicing the air between us.

"Virgins are a dying breed"
she says as
a lump of soft meat
rolls onto the orange tile
and sprawls moist and warm
beneath her polished
toenails.

Crossing the line

I assume the position,
horizontal, spread-eagled
in front of you,
shiver from exposure, not dressed
enough for the altered climate
between us, teeth chattering, knuckles
white in your tightening grip.
As your posture mirrors mine,
prone, head to head,
we fall.

In these brief seconds since you crossed
the line between should and shouldn't,
your leap sucking me into its wake,
we slip from controlled comfort,
the plane where our meandering lifelines
blithely intersected, and your riddles
all come back: *You*, you often said,
the paradox of silk, strong and soft,
tangle of actions, rumple of thoughts
to unravel. smooth out, retie and refold.
And together we tidied me.

The plane's complacent roll
now a distant waver of innocent words,
you believe we can float here
in these clouds forever
but they're laced with holes
you've chosen to ignore. I dare
open my eyes, apprehend the solid earth
rushing up to claim us.

Free fall exhilarates, surprising
as a kiss, but gravity accelerates
a body to response: foolhardy,
some one has to save us. Oh, you did
prepare me — *paradox of silk* —
if I unfold myself completely
you can ride me
like a parachute.

The Driver

A set of headlights throws his shadow on the dash,
outline of head and torso sliding onto the highway

and back again — breathing in and out,
like Jesse asleep beside him, hands folded over

her belly's gentle swell. Nights like these,
driving the dark to its outskirts, he can feel regret

rising like heat from that sleeping body;
unspoken desires fluttering behind eyelids

blue-veined and delicate as the wings of moths.
He drives this road over and over, her whole life

cupped in his hands, beating in his blood as he
grips the wheel. Over and over, he asks oncoming lights

to show her to him; and yet he finds
no shape but his own, mapped against the endless road.

Champion

During the storms of my seventh year, I learned to swim in the basement. The pipes all cracked and water filled the room like one of Father's bad tempers. I was a very late beginner. Mother bailed aimlessly as I learned to frog-kick and crawl, her thick thighs safely within reach. Jellyfish stung our limbs and sea-gulls dove from the rafters to peck at the seaweed on our heads. "Everything's all broke," Mother sighed as she tried to rescue the little logs of corn that floated around us for dinner. My small body was as purple as the rings under her tired eyes. Upstairs, Father paced, his raging getting louder. That year I became a champion swimmer. Mother threw me fish to help me grow and become strong.

"Life has been a bed of roses" (Not)

I figure you can always learn something from T.V.
like yesterday, on the Oprah Winfrey show,
the "Light my fire" seminar lady suggests
(to renew a dormant love-affair)
"cover the bed with rose petals
and make love on top if it" — but tonight,
just before dusk, limp cherry blossoms
lie on the grass, cover the cement path
to the backyard; and soon you will walk through
the open gate, stirring up the strewn petals with
your leather shoes, scuffing their maroon
shine with damp pink — the way you walk
out of my bed every morning, leaving
the scent of bruised petals in your wake.

JULIE PAUL

One Way to Please You

If I could climb up onto the bridge of your nose
and hold onto your ears while I straddled the bump you got playing hockey,
then what would I see if I looked into your eyes?

Being small enough to ride your face
the way kids ride animals and rocket ships in shopping malls,
would you swat me away before I deposited the fee?
And what would you charge me?

If I had enough, which I wouldn't,
I would stay there a long, long time,
past when the janitors came in to sweep up,
after the lights went out, long after
the neon and Musak were turned off.

And I would look from eye to eye,
back and forth
so that my head would appear in one,
then the other
        left   right
        left   right
swinging my small body like a pen-
dulum in front of your glassy stare

And then I would choose one,
the way you always looked at only one of my eyes
when you talked to me, like
there was something wrong
with the other, or the way
you kissed my left breast more than my right, it being
smaller, more compact,
just your size.

I would pick one eye,
and pulling the shade on the other,
I would crawl inside and stay
as still as an eyelash and wait until you felt something, and
your eye rolled around like a number
on a digital clock (I've seen them do that, me lying still and you in
me, looking every way but mine)
and then, with a quick dive
I'd get inside your head,
and take your muscles into my hands like reins
and I would have control
of where you looked
and what you saw
and I would be complete-
ly out of your sight, ju
(st) li(k)e you
said you
wanted.

Blood Drumming

A great-uncle,
burned down his hardware store.
Ran out of the flames black,
breathing smoke,
swinging a pick-axe.
Found some cows, sat down to dinner.
was buried twelve years later
on the grounds of an Ottawa asylum.

An aunt,
Wore three pairs of glasses at once,
had been a Vogue cover in 1931.
Carried howling vodka
from an apartment on Oriole Parkway,
mouldering apple pie
under Edwardian sofas
piled with ten year old copies of the Globe
    — don't touch those, I haven't finished reading them.
    And don't open the drapes, my skin! my skin!

Swords in a lakefront motel,
January in Thunder Bay.
Cold made steel insane.
Brains cobwebbed by cheap speed,
cousin Anthony does life.

My old man's stories.
Like a coroner's report,
he listed every detail
— weight, distinguishing scars,
dates of incarceration
and internment.

A derelict schoolmaster
giving rote lessons
year after year,
memory outlasting
his sight,
hearing
him.

History, geography,
The final exam:
who can name
all the flavours of death
in his own blood?

The Pause That Refreshes

Can this be the New Yorker?

Poems, cartoons, stories
articles about Russia, Sylvia Plath, President Clinton, even
Farley Mowat and Canada, but
what's this?

a full-page photo of a laughing woman,
smooth pink complexion, few visible wrinkles,
white hair
kneeling without stiffness to dig her
chrysanthemum bed.

Across the page a banner
black letters on peach ground:
YOU CAN FEEL BETTER ABOUT
MENOPAUSE RIGHT DOWN TO YOUR BONES.

Feeling better already, I conjure
a woman called Pamela
who rises from her chrysanthemum bed:
time for her support group meeting where
everyone will discuss
Estraderm Estradiol Transdermal Systems,
one friend saying, "I nearly bled to death every month
before I stopped . . ."
and another, "When HE
told me I'd go on having a period every month if
I took estrogen, I told him to bugger off.
You'd think
I'd said I didn't like being a woman
that I didn't like HIM."

"It's a patch," says Pamela, our gardening friend,
"You stick it on your ass."

Pamela remembers
a Life Drawing class
a couple of years ago.
The model was
a sappy young woman
whose tampax string
dangled like a shoe lace,
showed when she bent over.

No one mentioned it.
What could you say?

As Pamela drew the model
great warm gushes
bloomed between her legs
like a river flooding its banks.

Fear made her gestures large.
Soft black strokes of her charcoal
swept to the top of her paper
slipped off the sides so her picture was like a window
that couldn't contain the view
like Alice growing huge in Wonderland
when she drank the bottle on the little table.
Then Pamela's drawing
settled into its new form.

The instructor
a well-known (male) practitioner of pastels
noticed Pamela for the first time:
"Quite original. Carry On."

Pamela scurried to the washroom
not daring to look behind
at blobs of thick blood
brightening the institutional grey floor.

Rustling with paper towels and bathed
in an embarrassed, as well as hot, flush
she returned,
finished her superb drawing,
still has it,
framed.

It was just
a funny story Pamela told her daughter.
Not the sort of thing
you'd expect to hear
outside Homemaker's Magazine.
But now, the New Yorker!

So Pamela has started taking estrogen, the pre-
                                patch kind.

Her chrysanthemums,
fiery autumn bloomers,
thrive.

Unikkaatuat:
The Domestication of the Inuit Sea Spirit

(from a Montreal exhibition of stone cut prints by Peter Pitseolak at the McCord Museum)

1

Nuliayuk
the Sea Woman,
in these rooms of stone-cut prints,
is like Venus Anadyomene's
plain northern sister.

With a temper like a hockey player
she faces off against her father
mouth exploding
clouds of geometric Inuktituk
(sharp language of taboo).

That jolly brown dog with
patterned backpack
laughing mouth
red tongue
(the dog she married)

yaps as their ten puppies
gambol on the permafrost
chew boots
tug laces
shit on snow.

Nuliayuk's father scowls.
A dark myth unfolds.
Father and daughter
push off in their boat
on crayoned ultramarine. The father
tosses his daughter into spiked
scribbled waves. She clings to the gunwale,
he hacks off her fingers and thumbs.

Magical seals and walruses
spring from bloody floating stubs,
draw Nuliayuk back to the dog.

2

Nuliayuk and the dog live on an island.
they swim to shore for food.
When the puppies eat too much
they pack them in three canoes,
push them off to drift among ice floes.
The puppies become
Inuit, Indians, Kablunait.

And the spirit, Nuliayuk,
learns to punish with storms
breakers of taboo.

3

In these last
red, black, green pictures
pulled from the print-maker's stone
the Sea Spirit is
domesticated,
braids up her locks of passion,
travels by outboard motor canoe,
roars off on her *moto-neige*
with a whiff of exhaust
or aeroplane glue.

And the dog is
domesticated too
demoralized by boarding school,
out of a job,
drinks when he can get it and
goes to church.

Only at night
under moving organ pipes of
Northern lights
Nuliayuk and the dog
dance and
dream stone pictures.

———————

Note: The Sea Spirit, Nuliayuk, appears under many names in many different Inuit myths. In most versions she marries a dog and returns to punish the breakers of taboo. Peter Pitseolak, the Inuit artist from Southwest Baffin Island, has made a series of coloured drawings and stone prints illustrating the myth. In the Inuit *language,* Inuktituk, unikkaatuat *means* stories *and* kablunait *white men.*

Green Glass

Last night I dreamed I bought hundreds of green glass
plates from K-mart. *I don't need all these,*
I thought as I stood over the dining room
table where I'd laid them out
like circles of Burmese jade.
Once, years ago, walking down Fort Street
a green dessert plate caught my eye.
Displayed on gold
velvet, it was chipped and scratched and far
too expensive. *Even so*
said the boy beside me, *it has survived since the twenties.*
It was December and snowing the day
we stood at that antique
store window and felt ourselves
leaving the sidewalk, swimming with clasped hands
into a pool of green possibility. Finally
he went in and bought me the plate for some
ridiculous price and later we went back to his brother's
apartment overlooking a busy
intersection where I asked
over tea — would he like
to make love? I remember almost nothing
of this boy except that when he was
about to reach orgasm his arms shot out on either side
of his body, his fingers splaying like wing-tips.
For the next three days, traffic
slid in muffled silence
beneath us as we shuddered again
and again into collapse, his brief but recurring
readiness for take-off filling me with inexplicable
happiness. Last night in my dream
I bought all the 99 cent plates
in the store, in fact, I
dreamed I possessed every piece of green
glass in the world. When I think of that winter

I think of words such as *living*
and *faith*, of a bird
preparing for flight. I think of
that boy's body moving slowly above mine.
Though it never left earth, how it kept on believing.